CHIARA'S SWEET CROSS

A Book of Novenas
with Servant of God

Chiara Corbella Petrillo

Tilapia House publishes works of Christian thought in service of the Catholic Church, guided by the apostolic tradition of Saint Peter and committed to truth, piety, and fidelity.

TILAPIA

HOUSE

CHIARA'S SWEET CROSS

NOVENA LIST
The novenas available in this book are as follows:

Vocational & State-of-Life Intentions
Novena for My Vocation in Life
Novena for My Discernment of Marriage
Novena to Become a Priest or Religious
Novena for a Future Wife
Novena for a Future Husband
Novena for Our Engagement
Novena for the Sanctity of Our Marriage

Family & Children Intentions
Novena for Married Couples Seeking the Gift of a Child
A Mother's Novena for a Healthy Pregnancy
Novena for Parents' Healthy Pregnancy
Novena for a Safe Delivery of My Child
Parents' Novena for a Safe Delivery
Novena for Parents Experiencing a Miscarriage
Novena While Caring for a Sick Child
Novena for a Mother Experiencing Postpartum Depression
Novena for a Family Experiencing Primary Infertility
Novena for a Family Experiencing Secondary Infertility
Novena for Families Seeking to Adopt a Child

Suffering & Conversion Intentions
Novena for Healing from Cancer
Novena for Freedom From Addiction
Novena for Conversion of Heart in Illness
Novena for Those Living With Fear of Death
Novena for Families of the Terminally Ill
Novena for Peace at the Hour of Death

Faith & Spiritual Intention
Novena for Trust in Divine Providence
Novena for Surrender to God's Will
Novena to Accept My Sweet Cross
Novena for Courage in Suffering
Novena for Hope When Life Feels Burdensome

HOW TO PRAY THE NOVENAS IN THIS BOOK

Each novena in this book follows the same simple and prayerful structure, uniting a meditation on the life of Servant of God Chiara Corbella Petrillo with a specific intention.

To pray one of the novenas in this book, proceed as follows:

1. Select a novena intention from the Novena List at the beginning of the book.

2. Begin with Day One and read the meditation for the day on the life of Servant of God Chiara Corbella Petrillo. The page numbers for the novena days are located on the next page.

3. At the conclusion of the day's meditation, you will find a list of novena prayers with corresponding page numbers. Locate the prayer that matches your chosen intention and proceed to that page.

4. Your novena concludes with the **Prayer for the Beatification of Servant of God Chiara Corbella Petrillo**, followed by an **Our Father, Hail Mary**, and **Glory Be**.

5. Follow steps 2 through 4 each day until you come to the ninth day.

This same order is followed for nine consecutive days, moving day by day through the meditations while praying the same novena intention each day.

May he grant you your heart's desire and fulfill all your plans… May the Lord fulfill all your petitions!

Psalm 20:5-6

"Chiara… this yoke, this cross…
is it truly as sweet as Jesus promised?"

"Yes, Enrico. It is very sweet."

DAY ONE

The Hidden Years of Grace

INVOCATION

*In the name of the Father, and of the Son,
and of the Holy Spirit. Amen.*

**Servant of God Chiara Corbella Petrillo,
faithful bride, mother, and witness to joy, pray for us.**

MEDITATION

Chiara Corbella was born in Rome on January 9, 1984. Hers was a childhood marked not by noise or extravagance but by the quiet constancy of faith. In the Renewal in the Spirit community, she learned early to fold her hands in prayer and to see every breath, every day, as a gift. She was the younger of two sisters, and those who knew her as a girl recall her instinctive gentleness. Even at the family table, she would sometimes hand her plate to her sister Elisa so that Elisa might eat first. It was a small gesture, easily overlooked, yet it revealed a heart already leaning outward in love.

Chiara loved beauty. She studied piano, then violin, and she liked to draw. She carried herself with a quiet dignity, not the firebrand of rebellion but the steady flame of a girl who somehow knew her life had purpose. And yet she was timid. She dreaded speaking exams at school, even when she was fully prepared. Later, she would admit this with a kind of disarming honesty: courage was not natural to her. Which makes her later heroism all the more striking—it was not her own strength, but God's grace, that reshaped her fear into courage.

Her faith in those years was like a seed beneath the soil—present, alive, but hidden. She breathed it in as one breathes the air of a family home, more received than chosen. But God was already at work, planting deep roots for the vocation He would give her: to show the world His love in the ordinary way of marriage and family.

In the summer of 2002, at just eighteen, Chiara traveled with friends to Croatia. Elisa was nearby in Medjugorje, so

Chiara decided to visit. That simple choice altered the whole course of her life. It was there she met Enrico Petrillo, a twenty-three-year-old on pilgrimage with his prayer group. They sat at the same table for a meal. Nothing dramatic, no thunderclap or vision. And yet both knew with a quiet certainty: their lives had crossed for a reason.

Chiara returned to Rome that summer changed. She could not yet see the road ahead, but she had taken her first step onto it. The shy girl would become a woman of astonishing courage. The generous child would become a mother who gave everything. The faith-like atmosphere would become her lifeline in suffering. And beside her would be the man who shared both her laughter and her cross.

Chiara Corbella's early life was not filled with extraordinary signs. It was shaped by small fidelities, hidden acts of love, and quiet willingness to let God lead. This is where holiness always begins: not in the great gesture, but in the ordinary moment offered with extraordinary love.

NOVENA PRAYERS

DAY TWO

God's Timing

INVOCATION

In the name of the Father, and of the Son,
and of the Holy Spirit. Amen.

Servant of God Chiara Corbella Petrillo,
faithful bride, mother, and witness to joy, pray for us.

MEDITATION

Chiara and Enrico began their love story in Rome. Their hearts were young and unguarded, full of warmth and sudden storms. It was the kind of love that could wound and heal in the same breath, that could quarrel in the morning and laugh again before nightfall. They entered a relationship that stretched across six long years, a pilgrimage of parting and return, of distance and discovery. They broke apart and found one another again more than once. Both carried hidden wounds they could not yet name. Enrico had lost his father when he was young; his loss had hardened into armor, his grief had made him cautious. Chiara's shyness taught her to guard her tenderness, fearful of being seen too closely and abandoned too readily. Their love was fragile, imperfect, and of this world, not yet sanctified by sacramental grace, yet God Himself was going before them, was with them, never leaving them or forsaking them.

In 2006, four years after their first meeting in Medjugorje, their love story ended one more time and this time appeared to be the final chapter of their story together. Chiara went back to Medjugorje alone. She climbed Podbrdo Hill with slow steps, her hands touching the stones still warm from the sun. She did not pray for answers. She prayed to let go. Her heart, tired from striving, laid itself down before God. What came to her was not a vision or a voice from Heaven but quiet words in her heart. *Wait... Trust...*

The songs of her childhood no longer satisfied the new hunger awakening within her. The bright flame of her early faith was deepening into something quieter, something rooted.

During Advent, she traveled to Assisi, the city where Saint Francis had found joy in holy poverty. Beneath the dome of the Basilica of Saint Mary of the Angels, she attended a retreat for young people seeking their vocation. She listened, she wrote, she prayed. The girl she had been still lingered within her, shy and bright, but now the woman was beginning to rise.

There she met Father Vito d'Amato, a Franciscan friar who heard her confession. His words were few, yet they carried warmth and weight. When he lifted his hand in absolution, peace moved through her like sunlight shining into dark water. It did not explain itself. It simply was. Before she left, she asked him to guide her as her spiritual father. He agreed. And from that day, Father Vito walked beside her as both shepherd and friend, a witness to her growing surrender.

In the spring of 2007, he gave her a verse to keep close. "When God opens a door, no one closes it. When God closes it, no one opens it." The words troubled her. They felt like both a promise and a warning. She prayed until her prayer became her surrender. Letting go was its own kind of dying, yet in dying she found a freedom that did not depend on understanding.

Enrico was searching too. He sought Father Vito as his own spiritual director, and in that meeting God's fatherly love began to weave their stories together again. When Chiara and Enrico met once more, they were not as before. Something in each had been stripped away. They were simpler now, readier, truer. The pain they bore as a consequence of the Fall was not gone, it was just easier to carry, because they were learning to help each other carry it. They began again, uncertain yet full of quiet hope. They decided to walk together toward God before walking toward marriage.

They joined the Franciscan March to Assisi, ten days and two hundred kilometers on foot. The road wound through valleys and rain, through laughter and fatigue. Each step became a small offering. Father Vito walked among them, silent and watchful, as grace continued its work. The journey revealed their hearts. Enrico's old bitterness rose up and showed its wounds. He began to see how grief had shaped him, how his pain had turned to blame, how he had hurt Chiara in the very places he was broken himself. Yet through her patience, he began to glimpse what love truly is. Chiara became for him what the San Damiano crucifix had been for Saint Francis, a mirror of divine love that suffers and saves at once.

On the sixth day of the march, they walked side by side beneath a fierce sun. The air shimmered with heat. Enrico turned to her and said they should end their engagement, then, without pause, asked her to marry him. She laughed, thinking the heat had made him delirious. He stepped from the path, plucked a sunflower, and placed it in her hand. "Let us marry," he said, his voice quiet and sure. His words carried the calm of a man who had stopped pushing against the door that God was opening.

Their long years of uncertainty had been a schooling in love. They had learned to forgive, to begin again, to trust what did not always feel tender. At last they were ready for the truth that sanctifies rather than flatters. They looked to Mary, the woman whose 'yes" held nothing back, and they offered their own "*fiat*" to God and to each other.

They were married in Assisi the following year. The morning was radiant, the bells loud and full. Joy trembled beside the foreknowledge of sorrow. Their vows were a promise of affection and a covenant made before Heaven. God's faithfulness sealed what their frailty could not. The years of trial had purified their love, cutting it down to its root, and from that root it bloomed again.

Marriage for Chiara and Enrico was a sign of God's faithfulness in the midst of human frailty. Their "I do" to one another was their "I do" to Him. Marriage was their path to sainthood, uniting two people into one flesh, two wills into one surrender, two suffering souls into one joyful song of praise. Chiara lived this truth each day. She kept her "I do" through laughter and through pain, through the radiant and the ruinous alike. She came to understand that love does not shield us from the Cross. It transfigures it. And in that transfiguration, even the Cross becomes sweet.

NOVENA PRAYERS

DAY THREE

The Fiat of Motherhood

INVOCATION

In the name of the Father, and of the Son,
and of the Holy Spirit. Amen.

Servant of God Chiara Corbella Petrillo,
faithful bride, mother, and witness to joy, pray for us.

MEDITATION

Chiara began her studies in political science at a small university near her home. Enrico spent his days in the hospital wards among the dying. He moved through rooms heavy with the scent of medicine and the sight of surrender, learning how to touch a hand that was loosening its hold on the world. Each patient became a teacher, each death a quiet revelation. The Lord who had joined them in marriage was leading them still. They could not see the road ahead, but they trusted that He would keep lighting the next step, even when the path turned dark.

Only one month had passed since their wedding when they learned that Chiara was with child. They traveled to Assisi, to the Portiuncula, where even the floor's ornate marble mosaic seemed to be a beautiful prayer. Kneeling together before the altar, they offered their child into the care of the Blessed Virgin. Their joy was simple and unguarded, radiant as sunlight upon trembling waters.

The first doctor's visit in October passed easily. Everything appeared normal. The life within her was strong.

The second appointment came after Christmas, on a morning of thin winter light. Enrico was in the hospital, recovering from surgery on his jaw, and Chiara went with her mother. The doctor traced the instrument across her abdomen and the screen came alive with movement. A small girl. Fourteen weeks. The room filled with wonder.

But then the air changed.

The doctor's eyes dimmed, her tone grew gentle. There was a malformation in the baby. She was missing a skull.

The medical word for this congenital malformation was *anencephaly*. There was no cure.

Time stopped. Chiara sat very still, her hands folded across her body, her eyes fixed on the fragile image of her child. The doctor spoke of the law, of what could be done, of how mercy sometimes means ending what has begun. But the doctor's voice became as distant as one speaking underwater while Chiara heard another language rising within her, words of Pope John Paul II (not yet Beatified) echoing through her memory, clear and piercing. No child is defective, though the world may be. Something within her steadied. Her eyes looked at her daughter again and she saw her—whole, beloved, chosen. The child lived now. She moved now. She was hers now. And Chiara knew what love required. She would carry her child as long as she could.

That night she lay awake alone. Enrico was still in the hospital. The silence around her felt vast and unanswering. She asked why, but Heaven gave no reply. Morning had come and she had wept until she could weep no more. The room felt hollow, as if even God had stepped back. On the table stood a small statue of the Blessed Virgin. Chiara looked at it through her tears. Some shift happened inside her. Peace entered her heart like light piercing through a cracked wall. She saw herself in Mary... Mary, who had carried life in the same womb and sorrow in her heart... Mary, who had gently blown on her Divine Son's skinned knee when He fell... Mary, who had walked beside Him on the Way of Sorrows and who had stood at the foot of the Cross and who had waited amid all her inconceivable heartache for His Resurrection. She had known and she had no doubt. And now Chiara knew and she must not fail in her faith.

When Enrico returned home, she told him. He listened quietly, his face steady, his eyes filled with tenderness. A heartbeat of silence passed until his swift words assured Chiara of God's miraculous hand at work in the soul of her spouse. "Do not worry," he said. "She is our daughter. We will accompany her as far as we can." They named her *Maria Grazia Letizia*—Mary, Grace, Joy. Each name was a promise. Each name was a prayer whispered Heavenward.

There were those who did not understand. Some called them naïve, others reckless. But the more the world questioned, the deeper they entered into the embrace of the Church. Father Vito remained near, reminding them that God Himself had opened this door that could not be closed by anyone.

The months that followed were hard. Chiara's body ached beneath the weight of life and loss entwined. Each movement was a surrender, each breath a prayer, while the grace of God dwelled with them in the suffering until gift and pain became one and the same. Their only petition was simple. That Maria might be born alive, that she might be baptized before returning home to God.

On the tenth of June, 2009, the hour had come. Chiara went into labor. The birth was swift. The child was placed in her arms, warm and breathing. Enrico bent close, his face beside theirs, his tears falling softly on the tiny brow. Father Vito arrived and poured the baptismal water over the child's head. She belonged now to Him who had given her to them. And now they were giving her back to Him. Maria Grazia Letizia lived for thirty minutes. It was long enough to be loved, long enough to be known, long enough to be a saint of the smallest kind.

Two days later they came to the church dressed in white. Enrico carried his guitar. Chiara carried her violin. Together they sang of the Resurrection. The air trembled with their song. There was no despair, only a quiet joy that felt older than sorrow. "If I had aborted her," Chiara said, "I would have tried to forget that day. Instead, it is one of the most beautiful days of my life. We experienced eternity."

The brief life of Maria Grazia Letizia gave Chiara and Enrico a taste of how much God loves bringing life into this world and how much grief pierces His Sacred Heart at the loss of a solitary innocent. Children are not possessions. They are mysteries entrusted to us for such a small space of time. The measure of a single life cannot be truly counted in the minute hand or by the fleeting hours that hurry by like seconds, but by the *fiat*—the "I do"—of the Creator who opens the door without counting the cost and we precious cocreators whose childlike help holds open His costly door, even against the death throes of the world. Chiara's "I do" to Enrico on their wedding day was her "I do" for all her children.

NOVENA PRAYERS

DAY FOUR

A Mother's Second Fiat

INVOCATION

*In the name of the Father, and of the Son,
and of the Holy Spirit. Amen.*

**Servant of God Chiara Corbella Petrillo,
faithful bride, mother, and witness to joy, pray for us.**

MEDITATION

Chiara and Enrico returned to Medjugorje with Father Vito not long after their daughter, Maria Grazia Letizia, had been born and baptized and surrendered back to God the Father. Chiara and Enrico did not come to mourn. They came to give thanks. They came to lay the brief radiance of their daughter's life into the heart of the Lord who had given her. Kneeling again among the stones of that familiar hill, they prayed not for understanding, but for faith and for fruitfulness. They asked for another child.

Only a few months passed before God granted their prayer. Chiara was with child once more.

The first ultrasound showed the bright image of a healthy child on the monitor. The heartbeat looked strong. Chiara and Enrico could not deny the relief they felt, but they were also cautious.

The second ultrasound appointment near Christmas showed that the healthy child was continuing to grow stronger. Friends and family rejoiced. Some called this little one the child who would console them after their sorrow and make them forget the pain of their daughter's death. But such a thought was revolting to Chiara and Enrico. Forgetting was not their hope. Love for a new child could never overshadow love for another child. This second child that God had given to them only deepened their love for their first.

Then came the third ultrasound. The air in the examination room was still and cold. The doctor's face was grave as she moved the instrument across Chiara's belly.

The image on the monitor flickered and trembled. The screen showed their child, alive yet incomplete—one leg was missing, the other ended in a small stump. The doctor said nothing. The room fell into silence. Enrico stared. Chiara closed her eyes. The serenity on her face was betrayed only by the sheen of the two tear streaks down her cheek. She and Enrico looked into one another's eyes. Between them passed a quiet recognition. The cross had returned. Different in form, but not in weight.

More tests followed. Each one revealed a deeper sorrow. The child in her womb had no kidneys and no bladder and the lungs were too small to draw breath. Yet there was a heartbeat. The child was a boy. Their son. His illness had no name. The doctors gave it none. They only understood that there was no medical connection between the death of the first child and the malady of the second. The only similarity between the medical conditions of their first and second child was that they would end the same way. Their son, like their daughter, would not remain long in this world. Perhaps a few minutes at most.

Chiara and Enrico knew all the reasons were bound together in the mystery of God's unfailing love. It was the same sacred thread that had always held them. Again came the offer of termination, spoken in the tone of mercy the world understands but Heaven never will. Again they refused. Their son would live as long as God desired. He would be born. He would be baptized. She and Enrico named him Davide Giovanni.

Faith did not make Chiara untouched by fear. She lived her pain fully. She questioned and she wept. But she did not let her heartache harden into rebellion. She spoke to God as to one who listens. She wrestled with Him and waited for His answer. His reply was always peace. It came like light returning at dawn after the night has done its worst.

Together she and Enrico took again the narrow road of trust, the one that leads always toward the Cross. They no longer asked why. The silence of God was enough for them because His silence was not a sign of His absence, but of His abiding right beside them—as a husband sits wordless beside his bride. Their peace no longer depended on the lifting of sorrow. It was born within sorrow itself. When people asked about her pregnancy, Chiara smiled and said their son had a meeting with God in Paradise after he was born.

Chiara and Enrico's path led them to the ancient church of Sant'Anastasia, where the relics of Saint Joseph's cloak and the Virgin's veil are kept and where the Eucharistic Lord abides in perpetual Adoration. Chiara and Enrico laid their son upon the altar of His mercy and renewed their *fiat*.

Chiara and Enrico could have turned inward, could have become as innocently selfish as a wounded animal licking at the pain in the hope of relief. But that was not their way. They opened their home and invited family and friends to pray and eat and spend time together. Their table became a place of prayer. Thursday evenings were filled with good souls who came burdened and left lighter. Chiara's serenity left no space for despair. She never tried to explain God. She trusted Him. That trust became her witness.

Father Vito often came from Assisi to visit them. Chiara's joy shone like spring sunlight through the windows. They prayed together and spoke of the Will of God in their lives. Grace filled every room in the house. Peace lingered like a fragrance. Chiara's arguments with God diminished. She was a daughter walking beside her Father, her hand in His, crossing a street full of noise and danger, unafraid. Trusting.

Not long after, Chiara and Enrico traveled north to Turin for the exposition of the Holy Shroud. Standing before the linen marked with the form of the Crucified, they prayed for strength to receive what Heaven would send. Enrico's mind turned to the passage in the Acts of the Apostles when the shadow of Saint Peter healed the sick. Enrico looked upon the shadow of the Savior upon the miraculous cloth and he knew that His shadow was now resting upon them both.

On the feast of the Nativity of Saint John the Baptist, Chiara went into labor. Enrico called Father Vito and asked him to meet them at the Fatebenefratelli Hospital, the place founded long ago by Saint John of God and his brothers of mercy. Father Vito hurried from the friary in Assisi but soon became caught in traffic. He abandoned his car on the side of the road and waved down a young man on a Vespa scooter. Father Vito explained the situation to him and the man moved forward in the seat and offered the Franciscan priest a ride on the back of the scooter. The man's name was Francesco. Father Vito smiled at the plans of Divine Providence.

Chiara's labor was swift. Before she knew it, she was holding her son against her chest with the cord still binding them. She whispered to him, "My son... My love..." He was beautiful. His curls were soft, his face at rest, his eyes closed as if dreaming. Enrico bent close. Father Vito arrived in time to pour the baptismal water over the child's head and trace the sign of the Cross. The heartbeat slowed. The breathing softened. Davide Giovanni Petrillo lived thirty-eight minutes. Chiara held him close until the stillness came. Heaven itself had bent low to gather him. Davide Giovanni had fought the good fight and had finished the race and his mother and father had kept the faith.

Two days later, they laid their son to rest beside their daughter at Sant'Angelo in Pescheria. Maria Grazia Letizia and Davide Giovanni, sister and brother, together. The gathering in the church was small but steadfast, a family of souls who had learned from them what it means to walk with God in sorrow and in peace. Chiara and Enrico once more wore white. They sang again of the Resurrection. Father Vito acknowledged that they were standing exactly one year later in the same place for the same reason according to the loving governance of God. Two pregnancies, medically unconnected, yet joined mysteriously in grace. Two children, brief in this world, yet profound with witness. God speaks through such things. He walks on the sea and then calls us into the storm. Chiara and Enrico were like the Shroud of Turin filled with the signs of Wounds and Resurrection for all eyes to look upon. Chiara smiled and said that she was happier now than she had been on her wedding day.

NOVENA PRAYERS

DAY FIVE

Choosing the Order of Love

INVOCATION

In the name of the Father, and of the Son,
and of the Holy Spirit. Amen.

Servant of God Chiara Corbella Petrillo,
faithful bride, mother, and witness to joy, pray for us.

MEDITATION

Chiara and Enrico set out on the pilgrimage of the Seven Churches in September when vestiges of hot Roman summers ebb before autumn's approach. They walked with candles in their hands and prayer on their lips. The pilgrimage took them all day and night as they walked twelve and a half miles across the city. They stopped at each of the seven great basilicas. The road had been long and now the cool air of the basilicas smelled of clean stone and ancient dust. The Basilica of Santa Maria Maggiore was an important stop for them because there they knelt before the relic of the Manger of Our Lord. Chiara and Enrico asked God to open a door that no one could close by allowing them to have a child that would live and move and have being.

God heard and allowed a few days to pass. Then Chiara learned she was with child again. They did not even know if this child would be a boy or a girl but Enrico seemed to have a good sense because he smiled and said, "We will name him Francesco."

They were at peace, but they were not without vigilance. What had been would never leave them. They knew the risks and the ache that comes with hope. Still, they walked forward in faith.

Not much time passed after that when a small sore began to sting Chiara's tongue. She thought little of it at first. Weeks passed and the sore grew into a wound. She went to the dentist. Then to a dermatologist. Then to an ear and throat doctor. He told her to have a biopsy.

There was joy in the meantime. The first ultrasound showed an excellent image of the child. The doctor said she had rarely seen an image so clear and strong. Chiara smiled. Enrico laughed.

But the biopsy from the wound on Chiara's tongue gave no clear answer. The wound grew into a larger lesion. Chiara underwent a small surgery that put the child in her womb into no danger. In the white light of the cold operating room, she clung to the rosary in her hand and she prayed from her heart as the doctors inserted instruments into her mouth and cut into her tongue.

The surgical procedure left Chiara without the ability to speak for a short time. She could hardly swallow. Eating was impossible. She wrote on a scrap of paper and pleaded with the nurses for something stronger than Tylenol. The pain in her mouth was sharp and tearing. Her tongue constantly throbbed. But she was pregnant. Stronger medication might harm the child she carried. A deep pain of feeling abandoned by God began to weigh upon her. Doubt crept into her mind. Fear filled her heart. Her faith felt stretched to its breaking point. Her spirit felt as if being crushed. Her only prayer was a small word. Help. That night was terrible. The longest of her life.

Enrico arrived at first light. She had just fallen asleep. Her eyes batted open as he read out loud from a collection of early texts about Saint Francis and Saint Clare of Assisi and the Franciscan movement in those early years. The Italian book was titled *Fonti Francescane*. The passage was about the *perfect joy* that Saint Francis unearthed through his poverty and his suffering and his total trust in God's love for all creatures, especially those burdened by the great weight of this brief life. Perfect joy is loving God's Divine Will in the suffering that He asks us to take up and carry behind Him on the Via Dolorosa.

Chiara listened and she remembered that she was not alone. God's love had not left her. It was there in the pain in her mouth. It was there in the pain in her heart. It was there in her husband's voice. It was there in the child in her womb. Chiara closed her eyes. She was ready to go home.

Results from the surgery came back later that day. Its medical name was Squamous Cell Carcinoma. But its most common name was just Cancer. Chiara called it "the Dragon."

Her doctors would have told any other woman to abort her healthy child and undergo a surgery that might eradicate the cancer and save her life, but they knew that such words would be ineffectual to the woman who had twice refused to abort children others had judged unworthy of even a breath. So her doctors told her that they could perform another operation after her child was born, but waiting that long would lessen her chances of survival. Then they provided the option of inducing labor as early as possible so that she could have the surgery sooner. They presented it as the best plan for her, but she knew that it was the worst plan for the child. Chiara would not take a risk on the life of her child for the chance to save her own. She decided that the second operation would come only after God revealed the hour of her labor. Not before. Her child was not a medical case up for debate or to take a risk upon. He was her son. "His name is Francesco," she told the doctors.

Each morning became its own offering. Each day was another step upon the long road of the Cross. Each evening brought her nearer to her own personal Golgotha, her own Place of the Skull. She walked it without complaint and she watched the child within her and she waited. She lived in the hope of holding a living child. "Another day," she said, smiling, "another thirty-eight grams for the baby."

Chiara and Enrico prayed throughout each day—the Rosary, the Divine Office, Lectio Divina. Their voices rose and fell in the horarium of the domestic church. They went to Assisi and knelt among the worn stones of the Portiuncula and they prayed with the Poor Clares of Gubbio, who spoke to God behind their grille.

In her notebook, Chiara wrote that God had made His people dwell in tents when they entered the Promised Land so that they might remember their true home was Heaven. She added that as the disciples on the road to Emmaus did not know the Lord at first, "so we did not recognize Him in this tumor."

The spring came early that year. The air was washed clean by rain. On May thirtieth, they rose before dawn. Rome lay quiet under a sky without clouds and shimmering with a universe of stars. They drove to Fatebenefratelli Hospital. Labor was not strong yet. They had enough time to sit in the small chapel and hear the Holy Mass. Early light entered through a high window and fell upon Chiara's folded hands. Then the hour came.

In the birthing room, machines hummed softly. Chiara remained calm. Prayer was in her heart. Enrico remained behind her, her left hand in his left hand, his other arm bracing her back. His eyes looked upon his bride with admiration and love.

Chiara later wrote:

> *The birth was slow, calm, and extremely sweet… Then, within the space of a few pushes, my little one came into the world and attached himself to me and began to suckle. This was the great gift I could not have with Maria and Davide. I was so happy to be able to give him what all mothers in nature give to their own children to make them strong.*

That evening, they wept together. The tears came softly, tears of thanks and of things unknown. The house was quiet. Outside, the city moved like something far away, a shadow under the night. They did not know what awaited them. They only knew who would walk beside them when the hour came.

Chiara held her son close. His breath was small and steady against her chest. She thanked God for the nine months that had brought him here, for the smell of her son in her arms, and for the cry that broke the silence and filled the room with life. She kissed the soft crown of his head. "Francesco," she whispered.

The wound in her mouth burned. It pulsed like a living thing. "The Dragon" was stirring deep inside. But she would not fight it tonight. This day was for her son. It was for his first sigh, his first cry, for the stillness that came after. It was for love, whole and unmeasured, quiet as the light fading through the window.

NOVENA PRAYERS

A. Vocational & State-of-Life Intentions

B. Family & Children Intentions

C. Suffering & Conversion Intentions

D. Faith & Spiritual Intention

DAY SIX

Life Borne Through Wounds

INVOCATION

In the name of the Father, and of the Son,
and of the Holy Spirit. Amen.

Servant of God Chiara Corbella Petrillo,
faithful bride, mother, and witness to joy, pray for us.

MEDITATION

Chiara held Francesco in her arms at last. The soft weight of him against her heart was both promise and farewell, both blessing and surrender. His breath warmed her skin, and for a moment time itself seemed to pause, as though heaven leaned close to listen. Yet even in that stillness, she knew what awaited her. The hour was coming soon for her to turn and face what she had named "the Dragon." The first lesion had been taken months earlier, but the battle was not finished.

Her thoughts went first to her son. She knew she might not be able to nurse him after the surgery. Her body, so newly given to life, would soon be claimed again—this time by wounds, by medicine, by the long climb back toward strength. So she asked two friends to be ready to feed him in her place. She smiled and called them "Francesco's wet nurses." Even that surrender was love. Her weakness did not diminish her motherhood, but rather revealed the secret depth of maternal strength that surrenders everything for the smallest life.

Four days after giving birth, Chiara was wheeled once more beneath the white glare of the operating room. The light was cold, almost cruel, sharp as judgment. When she handed her son to the nurse, tears broke free. That parting was the sharpest blade. The nurse carried the child to Enrico in the hall and surrounded by friends who read the Gospel of the day: "You will be sorrowful now, but your sorrow will turn into joy." Enrico led them to the little hospital chapel, where they knelt and placed Chiara into the pierced hands

41

of Christ. They prayed not for escape, but for endurance—trusting the One who had already entered their suffering and made it holy.

On the table, she slept under the hush of anesthesia, her rosary wound tightly around her hand. The beads pressed into her palm like small anchors in a storm. Machines murmured. The surgeons worked in measured silence. Somewhere within that white noise, her heart kept time—steady, obedient, alive. When the first test results were returned, the news was good.

But when she awoke, her face was swollen and her neck bound in gauze. Her voice was gone. The wounds of her suffering were visible to all who entered the room. Those who saw her said she looked as if she had just been crucified. Her body bore two passions at once—childbirth and the knife. Tubes wound across her arms. Bruises flowered purple on her skin. She lay as though caught between death and resurrection, the stillness of Holy Saturday made flesh—a mother pierced and silent, waiting beneath the shadow of the Cross.

The first hours were heavy with pain. It pressed on her chest like a great stone. She lay without strength, unable to lift her head. But when they placed Francesco into her arms, her heart steadied. She found she could nurse him after all. The child took life from her wounded body and, in the same instant, God poured life back into her soul. Two gifts from God met upon her breast—the giving and the receiving, both belonging to the same Love.

Father Vito observed: "A body like Chiara's, bearing such deep wounds and offering so much of itself, teaches us that one lives not because one breathes, but because one loves."

Not long after came the harder news. Two of the sixteen lymph nodes were found to be positive. The cancer had spread, quiet and swift. Chemotherapy and radiation would be necessary. Chiara listened and nodded. Her eyes did not dim. "If the Lord wants this," she said, "He will also give us the grace to carry it."

The hot Roman summer intensified the treatments that burned her skin. Her throat blistered, her mouth grew raw, and her voice thinned to a whisper. She vomited until her bones shook with weakness. And still, she smiled with that small, disarming humor that is sustained only by sanctity. "Now I finally know what morning sickness feels like," she said softly. Enrico laughed through his tears.

When swallowing became impossible, the doctors placed a feeding tube into her stomach. Each meal became a prayer. Before pressing the syringe, she waited for Enrico to bless the food, then whispered, "Here I am, Lord. I come to do Your will" (see Hebrews 10:9). Her nourishment was obedience. Her hunger was love.

Through every hour, she turned outward. She consoled her parents. She encouraged her friends. She cradled her son whenever her arms could hold him, refusing to let sorrow find a home near him. "I hope I can be here for at least his first ten years," she prayed. "In the meantime, Lord, help me to do my best today." Her prayer was always now—never later, never tomorrow. The present moment became her interior chapel.

When autumn came, the first course of treatment ended. Her voice began to return, weak but steady. Water on her tongue felt like a gift. Bread became a feast. The ordinary world, once forgotten, returned to her like a sacrament. She read the Catechism with Enrico. They prayed the Psalms at dusk while Francesco slept across her shoulder. Peace, patient and unassuming, came home to stay.

The days seemed almost ordinary again and that ordinariness was itself a blessing. She had faced the Dragon and stood, not unscarred, but unafraid. The future belonged to God. The present was full of His peace. Her husband, her son, her home—all were held within the chalice of her life, which she lifted with both hands and from which she drank deeply and gratefully. She lived gently within them, strong in faith, steadfast in hope, her heart resting in the love that endures suffering and calls it joy.

NOVENA PRAYERS

DAY SEVEN

At the Foot of the Cross

INVOCATION

In the name of the Father, and of the Son,
and of the Holy Spirit. Amen.

Servant of God Chiara Corbella Petrillo,
faithful bride, mother, and witness to joy, pray for us.

MEDITATION

Holy Week of 2012 arrived. The air was heavy with expectation, yet within that stillness came the news that silenced every illusion of safety. The tests had returned. The cancer had spread.

Chiara and Enrico received the truth as they had learned to receive all things from the hand of God. They did not soften it or hide behind the fragile panes of denial. Their peace was not born of ignorance, but of trust. They wrote to their friends with the calm of souls who had already surrendered. "Nothing more can be done," they said, "except to pray and to ask for the grace to live this trial with holiness." And then they added an invitation. They would return to Medjugorje—the place where they had first met, the place where their hearts had first been taught to entrust everything to the Virgin. "We shall not return empty-handed," Chiara wrote.

What began as a handful of companions became a small pilgrimage. Families joined. Friends joined. Priests, peers, parents and children all came. By the time they departed, nearly one hundred and seventy souls were with them. The airplane became a chapel in motion. Prayer beads whispered through the aisles. Laughter mingled with recited psalms. Beneath the cabin, in the quiet hold, rested a small cylinder of oxygen, ready in case Chiara weakened on the journey. Some noticed the white bandage covering her right eye because of worsening double vision. When children asked about it with unguarded innocence, Chiara made them giggle when she told them that she was a "masked pirate."

Her joy made even suffering seem weightless. The mood was reverent, tender, bright—a hymn that rose between sorrow and praise.

They reached Medjugorje and they spoke not of tragedy but of testimony. Together they told their story—their meeting, their marriage, the two children who had gone ahead of them into the Father's embrace, and the one now giggling in his father's arms. They spoke of a peace that does not erase grief but follows it, a serenity born from faith, rising quietly in the very soil where sorrow had once taken root. They did not ask for healing. They prayed for understanding. They prayed for constancy—to love, to trust, to believe until breath itself gave way to glory.

Chiara's body was frail, yet she insisted on climbing the rocky hill of Podbrdo. The stones were rough beneath her feet, but each step became a prayer. When she reached the summit, she leaned against the rail and gazed across the valley. Then she knelt before the statue of the Virgin. Those who saw her said she was unhurried, her face lifted in calm surrender. The woman who could no longer lift her child's bottle now stood smiling at the summit, her gaze fixed on Heaven.

The next day, they gathered for Mass in the small chapel of the Cenacolo Community. Families crowded the aisles. Children played at their parents' knees. The air smelled of clean stone and candle wax. Light entered through narrow windows and rested golden upon the wooden beams. There, before the altar, Chiara and Enrico renewed their vows. Their voices were low and steady. They placed a rosary and a small image of Mary into every hand and they echoed the words Christ spoke to His beloved disciple: "Behold your mother" (John 19:27).

They wanted their friends to understand why they had come. The Virgin was not an escape from suffering. She was a way through it. At the foot of every cross, she stands. Her silence steadies those who remain. Her presence does not erase pain—it fills it with purpose as she presents you to her Divine Son.

When the Holy Mass ended, they descended the hill in silence. The wind moved through the olive trees and carried the faint scent of rain. Behind them, the sky burned with evening light. Some whispered prayers. Others simply walked. Chiara moved slowly, her hand resting on Enrico's arm to keep her balance. Enrico carried Francesco on the other side, the three of them forming a living chain of faith, hope, and love.

The flight home was quiet and reflective. Chiara sat by the window, her face pale in the shifting light. Enrico's hand covered hers. She smiled. No words were necessary. They had come to give thanks. They had come to remember how to stand before the Cross. Now they returned to Rome, their own Calvary. Yet peace went with them. Chiara whispered to the Mother who had never left her, "Behold your daughter."

Days later, they went to St. Peter's Square for the Wednesday Audience with Pope Benedict XVI. The city gleamed in the sunlight of a cloudless day. The marble colonnades curved like open arms. The crowd murmured in many tongues, a living prayer rising toward Heaven. Chiara stood beneath the vast May sky, her body weakened but steady. Francesco, wrapped in white, slept in her arms. Enrico guided her gently through the crowd as the Swiss Guards led them forward.

When they reached the Holy Father, Enrico spoke quickly, his voice trembling. "Holy Father, my wife Chiara has cancer, but she postponed her treatment to give birth to our son, Francesco. Now she is terminal." The Pope listened. His face slowly softened as he took in all that was shared. For a moment, he said nothing. Then he reached out and laid his hands upon Chiara and the child and he drew them into his fatherly embrace. The square, crowded and alive, seemed to fall silent. Enrico placed a letter in the Pope's hands—a letter telling their story, their offering. The Holy Father nodded gently and blessed them before they were led away.

The sound of the crowd rose again like a wave, but within Enrico, something fell quiet. A burden he had carried was gone. He took Chiara's hand and they walked on in peace. All had been given. God had received it.

Chiara's hope in eternal life was not a flight from the world, but an anchor sunk deep within it. She believed Heaven was not far away but near, pressing against the thin veil of this life, waiting to be seen. Christ's promise sustained her: "I go to prepare a place for you" (John 14:3). Those words were enough. They did not erase her suffering. They made it holy. They taught her that pain could be endured, and so she endured it.

She looked to His Mother and placed herself, small and unarmed, into her care. Chiara did not pray to be spared. She prayed to be faithful. Grace to live. Grace to suffer. Grace to love. And when the hour came, grace to die as a disciple dies. Her prayer, refined in fire, became one single act of surrender—the prayer of Christ made her own: "Not my will, but Yours be done" (Luke 22:42).

NOVENA PRAYERS

DAY EIGHT

The Cross as Lampstand

INVOCATION

In the name of the Father, and of the Son,
and of the Holy Spirit. Amen.

Servant of God Chiara Corbella Petrillo,
faithful bride, mother, and witness to joy, pray for us.

MEDITATION

Chiara's illness deepened as spring leaned quietly into
summer. The pain sharpened like a blade being honed, and
her body, once so ready for life, grew light and fragile. Yet
within that frailty there rose a quieter strength, the kind that
grows only in those who have come to trust God completely.
She and Enrico left the noise of Rome behind and went into
the open countryside, bringing little Francesco with them.
They returned to her family's home near Manziana, a place
called *Pian della Carlotta*—the Plain of the Free Woman.
The house stood on a serene rise of land, surrounded by
fields that stretched out in long, green waves. The air
drifted with the scents of grass, pine, and distant sea. Wind
moved through the sycamore branches like gentle devotions
whispered by creation itself. This place became her refuge
in the last month of her life. It was here that beauty and
family and the steady procession of friends wrapped her in a
gentleness the world could not give.

A hospital bed was placed in the room where her
childhood memories rested like pressed flowers in a book.
Yet the room, marked by suffering, did not become a
sickroom. On a small table beside her bed stood a golden
tabernacle. The Eucharist dwelt there. Each day, the Holy
Mass was offered only a few feet from where she lay. Enrico
would later say, with tears and wonder, "To have the Lord at
home was an incredible gift." The space took on a stillness
that was not absence but presence. Even the air seemed to
wait with her, filled with a reverence deeper than silence.

People came not just from the nearby towns but from miles of winding roads, from cities and parishes, from unexpected corners of life. Some came to speak with her. Others came simply to sit at her side and place their own weary hearts near hers. They carried their fears, their questions, their grief—the heavy weights no one likes to name. Chiara was puzzled by their visits. "Why are they coming?" she asked softly. "What do they want from me? I have nothing to tell them." But she did not see what they saw. Her silence taught more than words. Her smile, shaped within pain, became a kind of sacramental. Those who entered her room bowed down beneath sorrow often left lighter, as though someone had lifted just enough of the burden for them to walk again. Many said the peace they carried away felt like the peace Simon of Cyrene must have known after touching the Cross of the Savior. Chiara drew her strength from God and she gave it away freely to everyone.

The Thursday Rosary that had once gathered a small circle of friends in Rome now rooted itself in the soil of *Pian della Carlotta*. At first, they prayed in the guesthouse—just a handful of voices rising like incense. Soon, the space could not hold them. Each week, nearly seventy people climbed the hill as the sun slipped behind the fields, carrying candles, food, and their unspoken hopes. They filled the main house. The sound of prayer mingled with the aroma of bread and soup drifting from the kitchen. Those evenings felt like the early days of the Church, when believers gathered in ordinary rooms, breaking bread with reverence and love.

When her strength allowed, Chiara sat among them. Her grandmother stayed close, holding her hand with the gentleness of someone who has lived long enough to understand the true gift of our short time together. And when the final prayer faded into silence and supper began, Chiara would lean toward her grandmother with a playful grin and whisper, "Nonna, stay beside me. We have the best excuse in the world to keep to our seats." Even in weakness, she carried a quiet joy, a small and holy humor. Her weariness itself had become a new way of loving.

Father Vito often came from the friary, driving the long road through the pines. He arrived in the late afternoons when the light lay golden across the fields. He led Adoration and Benediction, lifting the monstrance high and blessing the gathering with the radiant presence of Our Eucharistic Lord. In time, he asked his superiors for permission to remain with Chiara and Enrico through the remainder of their pilgrimage. Later, he said it had been a schooling in holiness—a place where love and suffering met face to face. "To see Chiara consumed by illness," he said, "and yet consumed by love for her husband and her son, makes me think of my Spouse, Christ, who gave His body for love."

The prayers in that house grew slower, deeper, more certain. Grace hung in the air like the first mist lifting from the sea at dawn. No one doubted God was near. He waited with them quietly, the way a faithful friend stays near one preparing for the long road home.

One evening, during the Holy Mass celebrated in her room, the Gospel of Matthew was read. The candles flickered against the white walls, the light trembling as though listening. The words fell with a clarity that seemed meant for her alone: "You are the light of the world. A city set on a hill cannot be hidden. Nor do men light a lamp and place it beneath a basket, but upon a stand, so that it may give light to all in the house" (Matthew 5:14-15). The words hung in the air, bright and weighty.

When the reading ended, Father Vito turned to her and asked, "What is the lampstand, Chiara?"

She lay still, her hands folded over the blanket. Her smile formed slowly, gently. Her voice was a thread of sound. "The lampstand," she whispered, "is the Cross."

The room held its breath. No one moved. In that moment, her answer revealed the heart of her holiness. Her suffering did not dim the light of God. It lifted it. Her illness, her frailty, her nearness to death—none of these concealed His glory. They became the lampstand upon which His light was raised for all to see. The Cross was not her defeat. It was her offering, her mystical wedding gift, her stained-glass window through which the radiance of Christ streamed unbroken into the world.

NOVENA PRAYERS

DAY NINE

The Art of a Holy Death

INVOCATION

In the name of the Father, and of the Son,
and of the Holy Spirit. Amen.

Servant of God Chiara Corbella Petrillo,
faithful bride, mother, and witness to joy, pray for us.

MEDITATION

Every Christian longs for a holy death, a passing reconciled with God and strengthened by the Sacraments, a departure wrapped in the love of those who remain. The heart hungers for such peace. It yearns for the quiet joy of a soul that dies as it has lived, resting in the mercy of the Father. The Church calls this longing the *ars moriendi*—the art of dying well. In Chiara Corbella Petrillo, this art was not a theory or a poetic phrase. It became flesh and bone. It became every inhale and exhale. It became a radiance no darkness could dim. Pain ripened into peace. Suffering unfolded into surrender. Surrender blossomed into sanctity.

At *Pian della Carlotta,* her final month moved with the slow, sacred rhythm of an ancient psalm prayed in the half-light of sunrise. The days carried both ache and calm. Outside, green fields lay beneath the vast Italian sky where clouds drifted like wandering petitions lifted toward God. Wind moved gently through the grass. Air from the nearby coast tasted faintly of brine. Within the house, time thinned. Eternity pressed softly upon it, not with fear, but with a quiet insistence as though Heaven drew near enough to feel. Love surrounded her on every side. Enrico remained always within reach, steady as a lit candle. When her strength allowed, they placed little Francesco into her arms, and he nestled against her with the trust of a child who knows nothing but love. Her parents sat close to her bed. Friends entered quietly through the old wooden door, dropping to their knees at the threshold or praying at her feet, reverent as pilgrims approaching a shrine.

In her room stood a golden tabernacle veiled in white and crowned with flowers. Within it dwelled the Eucharistic Presence whom she had adored since childhood. The sanctuary lamp flickered softly with the susurration of her Bridegroom, drawing near, summoning her in the silence: "Arise, my love, my beautiful one, and come away" (Song of Solomon 2:10). The Eucharist became the core of her final days. He steadied her. His Presence was the soothing balm pouring meaning and dignity into the depths of her wounds. And when her voice could no longer rise in prayer, the longing within her became its own quiet utterance, a wordless offering given wholly to the One her heart loved.

Her days followed the rhythm of the Holy Mass. Each morning when Father Vito lifted the Host, Chiara lifted her eyes. Her gaze held the love of the Mystical Bride to her Eternal Bridegroom. Adoration, communion, and silence wove themselves into her soul like threads in a tapestry woven according to Heaven's order. She no longer prayed to remain in this world. She prayed to be united with the Will that had shaped her childhood, her marriage, her motherhood, and her long suffering. Her body grew thin and her voice slight, but the fire within her only brightened. Her suffering became her altar. Her weakness became the monstrance through which Christ revealed Himself to all who witnessed the mystery of her dying.

On her last day, the air was filled with perfect stillness. The Eucharist remained near. She lay upon her bed as sunlight spilled in gentle gold across the sheets. Her breathing slowed into a series of small offerings, each one a small psalm of surrender. Enrico sat beside her. He had walked with her through every season—joy, loss, hope, fear, tenderness, and now this final threshold. He covered her hand with his own. His thoughts drifted to the words of Christ: "Come to me, all you who labor and are burdened, and I will give you rest… My yoke is sweet* and my burden is light" (Matthew 11:28-30).

He spoke the scripture aloud, breaking the quiet. After a moment, he looked at her, his voice barely a breath. "Chiara… this yoke, this cross… is it truly as sweet as Jesus promised?"

She turned her gaze from the tabernacle to her husband. For a moment, the shadow of pain seemed to fade away as the soft, tender rising of her lips formed a small smile. And with a voice that seemed carried on the breath of God, she whispered, "Yes, Enrico. It is very sweet."

On June 13th of the year 2012, at the age of twenty-eight, Chiara Corbella Petrillo surrendered her soul into the pierced, glorious hands of her Eternal Bridegroom.

At her funeral, she was arrayed in her wedding gown. The silk shone with a purity that felt almost unearthly. Her body was fragile, but her face glowed with a serenity that startled those who looked upon her. Without a word, they understood: her entire life had been an offering. A gift to her husband. A gift to her child. A gift to her parents and friends. A gift finally given back to her Divine Spouse. Her holy death was not an ending. It was a completion. It was the final step of a marriage begun on earth and now fulfilled in the Eternal Wedding Feast of the Lamb.

Tears filled every eye, yet despair found no place among them. Enrico spoke softly, his voice steady with the grace he had witnessed. "There is no greater miracle than peace in death."

That peace became Chiara's legacy. She showed that holiness does not flee from sorrow. Holiness walks into every sorrow, every agony, every heartache with our cross firmly upon our shoulder and the lamp of the soul held high. Holiness presses onward through the gloom of this fleeting world to illuminate the darkness in the simple steps of smiles and laughter and faith in the midst of fears. Holiness places all things into the hands of Christ and trusts Him to carry us across the threshold of Eternal Life.

*In English, Matthew 11:30 is often translated as "**For my yoke is easy and my burden is light.**" The word rendered here as "sweet" reflects the Italian translation familiar to Chiara and Enrico: «**Il mio giogo infatti è dolce e il mio carico leggero**». This nuance does not suggest that the Cross is effortless, but that it is gentle, fitting, and borne in love. It is in this sense that Chiara came to understand the Cross not as easy, but as sweet.

NOVENA PRAYERS

NOVENA PRAYERS

Vocational & State-of-Life Intentions

PRAYER FOR MY VOCATION IN LIFE

O God of Wisdom and Love, through the intercession of Your servant, Chiara Corbella Petrillo, who sought Your Divine Will with humility and trust, look with kindness upon me as I discern my vocation.

If it is Your will that I embrace the priesthood, religious life, or consecrated virginity, grant me clarity of mind, purity of heart, and the courage to offer You my whole life for the good of Your Church and for the salvation of souls.

If You desire that I live the vocation of holy marriage, prepare me to love with fidelity, sacrifice, and joy, that my life may become a witness to Your faithful and fruitful love in the world.

But if my path remains hidden for a time, grant me patience in waiting, peace in uncertainty, and the grace to trust that Your plan is always good and that You Yourself are my greatest treasure.

I ask this through the holy Name of Jesus, in the power of His Precious Blood, and by the glory of His Cross and Resurrection.

Amen.

Turn to the Beatification Prayer on page 115.

PRAYER FOR MY DISCERNMENT OF MARRIAGE

O God of Providence and Perfect Timing, through the intercession of Your servant, Chiara Corbella Petrillo, who learned to wait upon Your will with patience and peace, teach me to trust the path You have prepared for my life.

You know the longings of my heart— the quiet hopes, the hidden fears, the desire to give myself in love. Let my waiting become a prayer, my uncertainty a place of faith, and my longing a doorway through which Your grace may enter.

If it is Your will that I enter the vocation of marriage, prepare my heart to recognize Your gift and to receive it with reverence and freedom. Grant that I may love not only with emotion, but with fidelity of will and purity of heart. Form in me a love that serves, sacrifices, and forgives—a love born from Your Cross and strengthened by Your grace.

And if You call me to another path, let my heart rest in the certainty that You alone are enough. Teach me, like Chiara, to trust even when I am afraid, to surrender even when the way is unclear, and to love even when it costs.

May my life, whatever form it takes, become a witness that Your plans are always good and that every vocation is born from Love itself.

I ask this through the Holy Name of Jesus, in the power of His Precious Blood, and by the glory of His Cross and Resurrection.

Amen.

Turn to the Beatification Prayer on page 115.

PRAYER TO BECOME A PRIEST
OR RELIGIOUS

O God of All Wisdom and Love, through the intercession of Your servant, Chiara Corbella Petrillo, who gave her life wholly to Your will, grant me clarity and courage as I discern whether You are calling me to:

(*men*) priesthood or religious life.

(*women*) religious or consecrated life.

If this is Your desire for me, purify my heart of fear and self-seeking, and form within me a love strong enough to belong to You without reserve. Teach me to desire not status or security, but hidden fidelity, joyful sacrifice, and union with You alone.

If You call me to this path, give me the grace to say "yes" with freedom, to persevere in obedience, and to offer my life for the salvation of souls. May my vocation, lived in humility and truth, be a sign of Your mercy in the world.

I ask this through the Holy Name of Jesus, in the power of His Precious Blood, and by the glory of His Cross and Resurrection.

Amen.

Turn to the Beatification Prayer on page 115.

PRAYER FOR A FUTURE WIFE

O God of Providence and Tender Care, through the intercession of Your servant, Chiara Corbella Petrillo, who received her vocation to marriage with trust and surrender, I entrust to You the woman who will one day be my wife.

Even now, before we meet or recognize one another, pour Your grace upon her life. Strengthen her in virtue, guard her in purity, and deepen in her a heart attentive to Your voice. Give her peace in waiting, courage in fear, and joy in knowing she is loved by You.

Prepare me also for the vocation You desire. Purify my intentions, guide my choices, and make me ready to receive Your gift with reverence and freedom. Teach me to wait with patience, to trust Your timing, and to surrender every expectation to Your Divine Will.

When in Your wisdom our paths meet, may our union be marked by Your grace, our love rooted in Your truth, and our future shaped by Your plan for our lives. May our marriage, in Your perfect time, be a witness of fidelity, fruitfulness, and grace.

I ask this through the Holy Name of Jesus, in the power of His Precious Blood, and by the glory of His Cross and Resurrection.

Amen.

Turn to the Beatification Prayer on page 115.

PRAYER FOR MY FUTURE HUSBAND

O God of Providence and Tender Care, through the intercession of Your servant, Chiara Corbella Petrillo, who trusted Your timing in all things, I entrust to You the man whom You are preparing to be my husband.

Bless his heart, his faith, and his vocation. Guard him from discouragement and sin. Strengthen him in purity, courage, and perseverance. Shape him into a man after Your own Heart, so that when the day comes, our love may reflect Your love.

Prepare my heart as well, O Lord—to receive Your gift with humility, freedom, and joy. Teach me to wait with peace, to trust without fear, and to grow each day in the holiness that makes a woman capable of lifelong love.

In Your perfect time, unite our paths according to Your Divine Will. May our marriage, in Your perfect time, be a witness of fidelity, fruitfulness, and grace.

I ask this through the Holy Name of Jesus, in the power of His Precious Blood, and by the glory of His Cross and Resurrection.

Amen.

Turn to the Beatification Prayer on page 115.

PRAYER FOR OUR ENGAGEMENT

O God of Faithful Love, through the intercession of Your servant, Chiara Corbella Petrillo, who with Enrico learned that true love is born of surrender, bless our engagement and the path that leads us to the covenant of marriage.

Teach us to love with reverence and simplicity, to seek not to possess but to serve, and to build our joy upon the solid rock of Your Divine Will. Keep us pure in heart and steadfast in hope, that our love may be shaped by prayer and strengthened by grace.

As we prepare for marriage, help us to always remember that the wedding is only the threshold of our vocation and that every promise finds its meaning in the Cross. Through the Sacrament of Holy Matrimony, unite us in a love that is faithful, fruitful, and enduring, a living sign of Christ's union with His Church.

When trials arise, draw us back to prayer, to Your Word, and to the Holy Eucharist, and remind us that our strength comes from the grace that binds our hearts in You.

We ask this through the Holy Name of Jesus, in the power of His Precious Blood, and by the glory of His Cross and Resurrection.

Amen.

Turn to the Beatification Prayer on page 115.

PRAYER FOR THE SANCTITY
OF OUR MARRIAGE

O God of Eternal Love and Faithfulness, through the intercession of Your servant, Chiara Corbella Petrillo, who with her husband Enrico lived the beauty of Christian marriage in joy and in suffering, in life and in death, look with tenderness upon our marriage, united in Your covenant of grace.

Grant that our love may be steadfast amid the trials of life, our hearts open to forgiveness, and our union a living image of the love between Christ and His Church. In moments of weariness, renew our strength; in moments of discord, restore our peace; and in moments of joy, let us give You thanks together.

Teach us that marriage is not self-serving but self-giving, that the cross we carry together is sweet, and that our daily fidelity offered in silence is the narrow way that leads to holiness.

May our home be Your domestic church where life is reverenced, faith is celebrated, hope is nourished, and love is continually renewed.

We ask this through the Holy Name of Jesus, in the power of His Precious Blood, and by the glory of His Cross and Resurrection.

Amen.

Turn to the Beatification Prayer on page 115.

NOVENA PRAYERS

Family & Children Intentions

PRAYER FOR MARRIED COUPLES
SEEKING THE GIFT OF A CHILD

O God of Life and Compassion, through the intercession of Your servant, Chiara Corbella Petrillo, who received each of her children as a precious gift from Your hands, look with tenderness upon us as we long for the blessing of a child.

You know the hope that aches within our hearts and the tears we shed in secret. If it is Your Holy Will, grant us the grace to conceive and welcome new life, that our home may be filled with the joy of a child and our hearts with gratitude for Your generosity.

But if this gift is delayed or withheld, strengthen our trust in Your plan. Guard our hearts from discouragement. Fill our marriage with charity, unity, and peace. Let this longing draw us closer to one another and deeper into the mystery of Your Fatherly love.

Teach us childlike trust, that we may hope in You despite fear and surrender to Your wisdom without bitterness— knowing that You never withhold what leads us to holiness.

We ask this through the Holy Name of Jesus, in the power of His Precious Blood, and by the glory of His Cross and Resurrection.

Amen.

Turn to the Beatification Prayer on page 115.

A MOTHER'S PRAYER FOR
A HEALTHY PREGNANCY

O God of Life and Protection, through the intercession of Your servant, Chiara Corbella Petrillo, who entrusted her motherhood to Your providence, I place myself and the child within my womb into Your hands.

You know my hopes and my fears, my gratitude for this gift, and my longing to welcome this child. Guard the little life You have begun in me. Strengthen my body, calm my heart, and watch over every step of the child's growth beneath my heart.

If it is Your Divine Will, grant me a healthy pregnancy and a safe delivery, that my child may enter the world with joy and my motherhood become a hymn of thanksgiving to You.

But if trials come, sustain me with Your grace. Keep me from anxiety, from discouragement, and from fear. Teach me to rest in Your providence, to surrender each day into Your care, and to trust that You are present in every moment of this journey.

Protect my child, O Lord—body, mind, and soul. May this little one, created in Your image and likeness, be held always within Your tender mercy.

I ask this through the Holy Name of Jesus, in the power of His Precious Blood, and by the glory of His Cross and Resurrection.

Amen.

Turn to the Beatification Prayer on page 115.

PARENTS' PRAYER
FOR A HEALTHY PREGNANCY

O God of Life and Protection, through the intercession of Your servant, Chiara Corbella Petrillo, who entrusted each of her children entirely to Your care, look with love upon us and the child You have placed within our hearts and home.

Protect our little one, O Lord—body, mind, and soul. May this child, created in Your image and likeness, be sheltered always within Your tender mercy.

Grant our home peace and unity, and make of it a true domestic church—a dwelling protected by Your angels, a place where Your Word is honored, and a sanctuary where Your grace is welcomed.

If worries arise, calm them; if complications appear, guide every decision; and if our path becomes difficult, let Your grace carry us when we feel afraid.

May this season of waiting deepen our love for one another and draw us closer to You, who are the Author of life, the Guardian of families, and the faithful Keeper of every promise.

We ask this through the Holy Name of Jesus, in the power of His Precious Blood, and by the glory of His Cross and Resurrection.

Amen.

Turn to the Beatification Prayer on page 115.

MOTHER'S PRAYER FOR A SAFE DELIVERY

O God of Life and Protection, through the intercession of Your servant, Chiara Corbella Petrillo, who entrusted each of her children entirely to Your care, look with love upon us and the child You have placed within our hearts and home.

Protect our little one, O Lord—body, mind, and soul. May this child, created in Your image and likeness, be sheltered always within Your tender mercy.

Grant our home peace and unity, and make of it a true domestic church—a dwelling protected by Your angels, a place where Your Word is honored, and a sanctuary where Your grace is welcomed.

If worries arise, calm them; if complications appear, guide every decision; and if our path becomes difficult, let Your grace carry us when we feel afraid.

May this season of waiting deepen our love for one another and draw us closer to You, who are the Author of life, the Guardian of families, and the faithful Keeper of every promise.

We ask this through the Holy Name of Jesus, in the power of His Precious Blood, and by the glory of His Cross and Resurrection.

Amen.

Turn to the Beatification Prayer on page 115.

PARENTS' PRAYER FOR A SAFE DELIVERY

O God of Life and Compassion, through the intercession of Your servant Chiara Corbella Petrillo, look with compassion upon us as we await the birth of our child.

Bless our home as a domestic church, a sanctuary that adores You and cherishes life. Calm our fears and strengthen our trust.

As the hour of labor draws near, surround us with Your protection and grant wisdom and skill to all who will assist us.

Watch over mother and child with Your gentle care. Preserve their health and keep them safe beneath Your sheltering hand.

Guard our child especially—body, mind, and soul—and bring our little one safely into the world in the light of Your grace.

We ask this through the Holy Name of Jesus, in the power of His Precious Blood, and by the glory of His Cross and Resurrection.

Amen.

Turn to the Beatification Prayer on page 115.

PRAYER FOR PARENTS
EXPERIENCING A MISCARRIAGE

O God of Compassion and Eternal Life, through the intercession of Your servant, Chiara Corbella Petrillo, look with tenderness upon our family as we grieve the loss of our child.

The life You knitted together in the womb was entrusted to us for only a little while. As You now receive our child in Your Fatherly embrace, receive also our tears as prayers rising to Your Heart.

Though our child's life was brief, [*say name*] is loved with an everlasting love. Let this truth console our wounded hearts. Heal the pain that cannot be spoken, and strengthen our trust that our child now lives in the light of Your Face.

Draw us together as a family, united by love that death cannot diminish. Guard us from despair, restore peace to our home, and keep our hope fixed on the day when You will wipe every tear away and reunite us in Your Kingdom.

We ask this through the Holy Name of Jesus, in the power of His Precious Blood, and by the glory of His Cross and Resurrection.

Amen.

Turn to the Beatification Prayer on page 115.

PRAYER WHILE CARING FOR A SICK CHILD

O God of Mercy and Strength, through the intercession of Your servant, Chiara Corbella Petrillo, look with love upon our family as we care for our child in sickness and fragility.

You know the weight we carry and the love that sustains us. Grant us patience in exhaustion, courage in uncertainty, and hope when the road feels long.

Bless our child with Your protecting grace—body, mind, and soul. Bring comfort in suffering, peace in fear, and signs of Your Presence in every moment of frailty.

Let our home be a true domestic church, where compassion is shared, sacrifice is embraced, and love becomes a daily offering to You. Strengthen our unity as parents, and teach us to see Your face in the face of our child.

We ask this through the Holy Name of Jesus, in the power of His Precious Blood, and by the glory of His Cross and Resurrection.

Amen.

Turn to the Beatification Prayer on page 115.

PRAYER FOR A MOTHER SUFFERING POSTPARTUM DEPRESSION

O God of Light in Every Darkness, through the intercession of Your servant, Chiara Corbella Petrillo, look with mercy upon me as I walk through this difficult season after the birth of my child.

My body has given life, yet my heart feels heavy and tired My mind is troubled, my spirit wounded, and the joy I expected feels far away. Lord, meet me in this place where I feel weak and uncertain.

Hold me close with Your gentle presence. Steady my thoughts and calm my fears. Lift the weight that presses upon me, and restore to me the peace that only Your Heart can give.

Send Your Holy Spirit to renew my strength and surround me with those who will support me with patience, kindness, and understanding.

In Your time, bring me again to the joy of motherhood and let me rediscover the strength that comes from Your faithful love.

Bless my child and bless those who care for us in this time. Let their love be a reflection of Yours. Guard our home with unity and grace, and let no shadow steal the love You have planted here.

I ask this through the Holy Name of Jesus, in the power of His Precious Blood, and by the glory of His Cross and Resurrection.

Amen.

Turn to the Beatification Prayer on page 115.

PRAYER FOR A FAMILY EXPERIENCING PRIMARY INFERTILITY

O God of Hope and Tender Mercy,
through the intercession of Your servant,
Chiara Corbella Petrillo,
look with compassion upon our family.

You know the longing within our hearts—
the quiet ache, the hidden tears,
the desire to welcome a child into our home.
Receive our waiting as prayer
and our sorrow as an offering of love.

If it is Your Holy Will,
grant us the grace to conceive and bring forth new life,
that our home may rejoice in the gift of a child.
But if this gift is delayed or withheld,
strengthen our trust in Your Divine Plan
and keep our hearts united in peace.

Guard us from discouragement and bitterness.
Let hope, not fear, dwell within our home.
Teach us that our marriage, lived with fidelity and charity,
remains fruitful in Your eyes.

And make our home a true domestic church—
rich in prayer, generosity, and steadfast love.

We ask this through the Holy Name of Jesus,
in the power of His Precious Blood,
and by the glory of His Cross and Resurrection.

Amen.

Turn to the Beatification Prayer on page 115.

PRAYER FOR A FAMILY EXPERIENCING SECONDARY INFERTILITY

O God of Compassion and Faithfulness, through the intercession of Your servant, Chiara Corbella Petrillo, look with mercy upon our family.

We thank You for the child(ren) You have already entrusted to us, and we place before You the longing to welcome another little one into our home. If it is Your will, open the way for new life to join our family, and let our hope remain anchored in Your goodness.

But if this gift is delayed or withheld, strengthen our trust in Your Providence. Protect us from discouragement and from every fear that troubles the heart. Fill our home with unity, tenderness, and peace, that our family may reflect Your love regardless of its size. Make our home a true domestic church, where gratitude and hope endure together in the light of Your grace.

We ask this through the Holy Name of Jesus, in the power of His Precious Blood, and by the glory of His Cross and Resurrection.

Amen.

Turn to the Beatification Prayer on page 115.

PRAYER FOR FAMILIES SEEKING
TO ADOPT A CHILD

O God of Love and Divine Providence,
through the intercession of Your servant,
Chiara Corbella Petrillo,
who welcomed every life as a gift entrusted by You,
look with kindness upon our family
as we open our home to adoption.

You are the Father of the orphan
and the giver of every true family.
According to Your Holy Will,
lead us to the child You have prepared for us
and prepare that child to be received by us.

Grant us hearts ready to protect and nurture,
and grant us minds ready to understand and guide
this gift of life given to us
in Your time and by Your design.

May our home become a true domestic church,
where You are worshipped in spirit and in truth,
in imitation of the Holy Family.

We ask this through the Holy Name of Jesus,
in the power of His Precious Blood,
and by the glory of His Cross and Resurrection.

Amen.

Turn to the Beatification Prayer on page 115.

NOVENA PRAYERS

Suffering & Conversion Intentions

PRAYER FOR HEALING FROM CANCER

O God of Divine Mercy and Love, through the intercession of Your servant Chiara Corbella Petrillo, who bore her illness with joy and confidence in Your providence, look with compassion upon [*say name*], who suffers from cancer.

If it be Your will, grant a complete healing, even miraculously, so that through this sign of Your power, the Church may recognize Chiara among the saints and one day honor her at Your altars.

But if it is not Your will that [*say name*] be healed, grant him/her the grace to embrace this cross as Your gift, the grace of repentance and conversion of heart, the consolation of the sacraments of the Church, and the peace of entering into eternal life, where every tear will be wiped away.

We ask this through the holy Name of Jesus, in the power of His Precious Blood, and by the glory of His Cross and Resurrection.

Amen.

Turn to the Beatification Prayer on page 115.

PRAYER FOR FREEDOM FROM ADDICTION

O God of Mercy and Deliverance,
through the intercession of Your servant,
Chiara Corbella Petrillo,
look upon me in my struggle for freedom.

You know the chains that bind my heart,
the habits that wound my soul,
and the places where I feel powerless.
Do not let shame or discouragement rule me,
but let Your mercy be my strength.

Grant me the courage to take the next step,
the humility to seek help,
and the perseverance to rise after every fall.
When temptation draws near,
let Your Spirit defend me;
when despair weighs me down,
let Your truth lift me up.

Restore what has been damaged in me.
Heal my memory, my desires, and my will.
Let this struggle become a road to holiness,
and this weakness a place where Your grace abounds.

Lead me into true freedom—
freedom to love, to hope, and to live fully in You.

I ask this through the Holy Name of Jesus,
in the power of His Precious Blood,
and by the glory of His Cross and Resurrection.

Amen.

Turn to the Beatification Prayer on page 115.

PRAYER FOR CONVERSION OF HEART IN ILLNESS

O God of Mercy present in the Most Holy Eucharist, through the intercession of Your servant, Chiara Corbella Petrillo, who allowed suffering to draw her ever closer to Your Heart, look with compassion upon me in this time of illness.

In my weakness, lead me back to You. As I approach Your Eucharistic Presence, let Your grace purify my desires,
heal the wounds of my heart, and awaken in me a new longing for holiness. When fear unsettles me, give me Your peace; when anger rises, grant me patience; and when despair weighs me down, lift me up with the light that shines from Your altar.

If it is Your will, restore my health. But if this cross must remain, let it unite me more deeply to Your saving sacrifice made present in the Eucharist. May this trial convert my heart and renew my love for You.

I ask this through the Holy Name of Jesus, in the power of His Precious Blood, and by the glory of His Cross and Resurrection.

Amen.

Turn to the Beatification Prayer on page 115.

PRAYER FOR THOSE
LIVING WITH FEAR OF DEATH

O God of Eternal Life and Perfect Peace,
through the intercession of Your servant,
Chiara Corbella Petrillo,
who faced death with trust in Your promise,
look with mercy upon me
as I carry the weight of fear.

Calm the anxieties that trouble my mind
and soften the dread that shadows my heart.
Let the light of Christ's Resurrection
dispel my darkness
and restore my confidence in Your nearness and Your love.

Teach me to rest in Your providence—
to remember that nothing can separate me
from the love of Christ,
and that death itself is but a doorway
to the fullness of life in You.

Grant me peace in moments of panic,
courage in moments of weakness,
and hope that reaches beyond this world
to the joy You have prepared for Your children.

I ask this through the Holy Name of Jesus,
in the power of His Precious Blood,
and by the glory of His Cross and Resurrection.

Amen.

Turn to the Beatification Prayer on page 115.

PRAYER FOR FAMILIES OF THE
TERMINALLY ILL

O God of Mercy and Eternal Strength,
through the intercession of Your servant,
Chiara Corbella Petrillo,
look with compassion upon our family
as we accompany our loved one in terminal illness.

Fill our home with Your peace—
the peace the world cannot give.
Strengthen us when fear rises,
comfort us when sorrow deepens,
and keep us united in patience, tenderness, and love.
In moments of helplessness,
remind us that no suffering is unseen by You,
and no act of care is ever lost.

Grant our loved one courage and serenity;
free them from fear and pain.
Let Your presence be near in every moment,
as gentle as the light that falls from the Eucharist.
If healing is not Your will,
prepare their heart for the embrace of eternal life,
and prepare ours for the path of holy surrender.

We ask this through the Holy Name of Jesus,
in the power of His Precious Blood,
and by the glory of His Cross and Resurrection.

Amen.

Turn to the Beatification Prayer on page 115.

PRAYER FOR PEACE AT THE HOUR OF DEATH

O God of Eternal Mercy,
through the intercession of Your servant,
Chiara Corbella Petrillo,
who met her final hour with trust and serenity,
look with compassion upon me as I contemplate my death.

When my strength fails
and the shadows grow long,
let Your peace descend upon me
like the light that rests upon the Eucharist.
Free my heart from fear,
my mind from confusion,
and my soul from every attachment
that does not lead to You.

Grant that the Sacraments
may be my comfort and my shield,
and that the Name of Jesus
may be the final prayer upon my lips.
Let my passing be an act of trust,
a surrender into Your Fatherly hands,
and the doorway to everlasting joy.

Receive me, Lord,
as You received Chiara—
gentle, ready, and filled with hope.

I ask this through the Holy Name of Jesus,
in the power of His Precious Blood,
and by the glory of His Cross and Resurrection.

Amen.

Turn to the Beatification Prayer on page 115.

NOVENA PRAYERS

Faith & Spiritual Intention

PRAYER FOR TRUST IN DIVINE PROVIDENCE

O God of Perfect Wisdom and Tender Providence,
through the intercession of Your servant,
Chiara Corbella Petrillo,
who trusted You even when the path grew dark,
teach my heart to rest in the certainty of Your care.

You know what I fear
and what I cannot yet understand.
Calm my restless thoughts and
grant me the grace to surrender each day,
not with resignation
but with confidence in Your Fatherly love.

When anxieties rise,
let Your peace steady my soul.
When I cannot see the road ahead,
let Your Word be my light.
When Your Holy Will is for me to carry a sweet cross,
give me the courage to say "yes,"
as Chiara did,
with simplicity, trust, and love.

Make my life a quiet witness
that Your providence never fails
and Your plans are always for my good.

I ask this through the Holy Name of Jesus,
in the power of His Precious Blood,
and by the glory of His Cross and Resurrection.

Amen.

Turn to the Beatification Prayer on page 115.

PRAYER FOR SURRENDER TO GOD'S WILL

O God of Loving Wisdom,
through the intercession of Your servant,
Chiara Corbella Petrillo,
who learned to place her life entirely in Your hands,
teach me the grace of true surrender.

You know how tightly I cling
to my plans, my hopes, my understanding of what should be.
I confess my fear of letting go,
my desire to control what belongs to You alone.
Meet me there, Lord, not with reproach,
but with patience and mercy.

When Your Holy Will is hidden,
give me trust.
When You ask me to sacrifice,
give me the courage to say "yes"
without bitterness or delay.

Teach me that surrender is not defeat
but love freely offered,
not the loss of self
but the discovery of who I am in You.
May my life, like Chiara's,
become an offering placed upon the altar of Your providence.

I ask this through the Holy Name of Jesus,
in the power of His Precious Blood,
and by the glory of His Cross and Resurrection.

Amen.

Turn to the Beatification Prayer on page 115.

PRAYER TO ACCEPT MY SWEET CROSS

O God of Love made Crucified, through the intercession of Your servant Chiara Corbella Petrillo, grant me the grace to accept the sweet cross You have entrusted to me.

I do not ask that it be taken away, but that I may put it on my shoulder beside You. When it feels heavy, stay close. When I am tempted to set it down, help me to carry it onward, until You bring me where You will.

Let me discover, as Chiara did, that the cross borne in union with Christ is not bitterness but gift, not defeat but communion, not darkness but a path toward life.

May this cross, accepted in love, become the place where I am shaped, purified, and drawn closer to You, until even I can say with faith and peace, "Yes, Lord, it is sweet."

I ask this through the Holy Name of Jesus, in the power of His Precious Blood, and by the glory of His Cross and Resurrection.

Amen.

Turn to the Beatification Prayer on page 115.

PRAYER FOR COURAGE IN SUFFERING

O God who are near to the brokenhearted,
through the intercession of Your servant
Chiara Corbella Petrillo,
grant me courage in this hour of suffering.

Not the courage that denies pain,
but the courage that remains.
Not the strength that pretends all is well,
but the strength that trusts You are here.

When fear rises within me, steady my heart.
When my weakness is exposed, let Your grace be enough.
Teach me to face each moment as it comes,
without fleeing, without bitterness,
placing my life into Your hands.

Let my suffering, united to Christ,
become a place of truth and love.
Give me the courage to hope, to endure,
and to remain faithful
even when I cannot see the end.

May I learn, as Chiara did,
that courage is not the absence of fear,
but love that chooses to stay.

I ask this through the Holy Name of Jesus,
in the power of His Precious Blood,
and by the glory of His Cross and Resurrection.

Amen.

Turn to the Beatification Prayer on page 115.

PRAYER FOR HOPE
WHEN LIFE FEELS BURDENSOME

O God of steadfast love,
through the intercession of Your servant
Chiara Corbella Petrillo,
look upon me as life feels like a burden.

You see the weight I carry
and the weariness in my heart and mind.
When joy feels distant
and the road feels long,
keep hope alive within me.

Do not let me measure my life
by ease or success,
but by faithfulness to You.
Teach me to hope not in relief alone,
but in Your presence that does not leave.

When I am tempted to grow tired of waiting,
remind me that You are at work even in silence.
When my strength fails,
let hope rise—not from myself,
but from the Cross of Christ.

May I learn, as Chiara did,
that hope is not lightness of life,
but trust that love remains.

I ask this through the Holy Name of Jesus,
in the power of His Precious Blood,
and by the glory of His Cross and Resurrection.

Amen.

Turn to the Beatification Prayer on page 115.

BEATIFICATION PRAYER

Servant of God Chiara Corbella Petrillo

Prayer for the Beatification of
Servant of God Chiara Corbella Petrillo

O God, who are the source of all holiness, we thank You
for the witness of Servant of God Chiara Corbella Petrillo.
Through her joy in suffering and her trust in Your goodness,
she showed the beauty of a life given as a gift. Grant that
her example may inspire many to follow Christ with fidelity,
and, if it be Your will, glorify her among the saints, so that
all may know the power of Your love. We ask this through
Jesus Christ, Son of God and Son of Mary. Amen.

Our Father...
Hail Mary...
Glory Be...

Servant of God Chiara Corbella Petrillo,
faithful bride, mother, and witness to joy, pray for us.

In the name of the Father, and of the Son,
and of the Holy Spirit. Amen.

CHIARA'S SWEET CROSS

TILAPIA
HOUSE